10 SCRIPTURES
to KNOW ✝ by HEART
Women

JJ GUTIERREZ

Copyright© 2022 JJ Gutierrez Author
First Print 2022; updated 2024

Written and Designed by JJ Gutierrez Author.

ISBN: 9798842611676

Unless otherwise indicated, all Scripture quotations are from the NLT New Life Application Study Bible, Third Edition, copyright 2019 by Tyndale House Publishers. All rights reserved. Previous editions copyright 1988, 1989, 1990, 1991, 1993, 1996, 2004, 2007, 2013 by Tyndale House Publishers, Inc., Wheaton, IL 60189. All rights reserved.

ESV Scripture References: The ESV Study Bible, Lard Print, ESV Bible, copyright 2008 by Crossway. All rights reserved. The Holy Bible, English Standard Version (ESV), copyright 2001 by Crossway, a publishing ministry of Good News Publishers. All rights reserved. ESV TEXT Edition 2016.

AMP Scripture References: The Amplified Bible, copyright 1954, 1958, 1962, 1987 by The Lockman Foundation. All rights reserved. Used by permission. The Amplified Cross-Reference Bible Published by Zondervan, Grand Rapids, Michigan 49530, U.S.A.

Author JJ Gutierrez
Cover Design and Typesetting by JJ Gutierrez
Editing and Proofreading Katie Landers of www.integrityproofreading.com
Author Photo by Jessie Dinkins
Contact info: hello@jjgutierrezauthor.com

Dedication

To women, like me, who want to store God's Word deep in their hearts.

Hello, I'm JJ!
This is me!

I am a corporate-career-woman turned homeschool mom, writer, girls Bible teacher, and Blue Line Brides co-founder & ministry leader. I share a lovely two story home with my husband of 26 years and our teen daughter. Our two oldest daughters have entered into adulthood and we have grand babies. Being called Grammy is the best!

I am passionate about sharing God's Word with women and teen girls. Nothing is more powerful to transform lives than knowing Christ, and to know Him, we must read, study and memorize the Scriptures.

I accepted Jesus as my Savior 27 years ago, the best decision of my life! Every day since, I've been growing and changing in miraculous ways. I am a lifelong Bible student because nothing is more important to me than knowing God. His Word is my guiding light, my strength and my joy. See my testimony @ www.jjgutierrezauthor.com/get-to-know-jj/

Most days you'll catch me with my Bible open, listening to a podcast, writing words, & sipping iced tea with my sweet German Shepherd, Bella.

XO, JJ

Contents

"*I know no other single practice in the Christian life more rewarding, practically speaking, than memorizing Scripture. That's right. No other single discipline is more useful and rewarding than this. No other single exercise pays greater spiritual dividends! Your prayer life will be strengthened. You witnessing will be sharper and much more effective. Your counseling will be in demand. Your attitudes and outlook will begin to change. Your mind will become more alert and observant. Your confidence and assurance will be enhanced. Your faith will be solidified.*"

Chuck Swindol

Introduction

Sister in Christ, did you know God provided you with a weapon to carry on the battlefield of life? This weapon has more penetrating power, firepower, thrusting power or stabbing power than any earthly weapon. It goes deeper and further...able to divide the soul from spirit and the bone from marrow (Hebrews 4:12). It searches and knows the inner thoughts of mankind and it overpowers every single tactic of the enemy. Pastor Alistair Begg says, *"...like a surgeon's scalpel...able to cut right through all the outer layers and cut right into the heart of it all."* And for those who study and memorize it, it's immediately ready for use and it can be taken on the go.

The type of weapon God gives isn't a secret or left up to our imagination. It is clearly stated, *"...and take the sword of the Spirit, which is the Word of God"* (Ephesians 6:17). The Word of God is the weapon. At this point you might be asking yourself, *"How can a book be a weapon?"* To better understand, let's look at the three different Greek terms that are commonly translated into English as word. The first is *graphe* and it simply means the physical book itself - the leather-bound covering with your name etched on the bottom right hand corner and the printed words on the sheets of paper that make up the tangible Bible.

The second term and the most familiar is *logos*. In the Bible, it refers to the message or the meaning of The Book. Think of it as the all-encompassing and over-arching revelation of God. Jesus was referred to as logos in John 1:1, *"In the beginning the Word already existed. He was with God, and He was God."* Jesus Himself was God's message in human form. More than just words on paper, logos is what we read and study and hide in our hearts. It's how we know God and experience His power in our lives because logos is alive and active (Hebrews 4:12).

However, neither *graphe* nor *logos* are used to describe the Word of God in Ephesians 6:17. The correct Greek translation is *rhema* which means the spoken or declared Word. Dr. David Jeremiah phrases it this way, *"The rhema of God means 'a saying of God.' We could translate this verse this way: 'Take the sword of the Spirit, which is the saying of God."* It's incredibly important we fully comprehend that rhema is God's spoken Word. Not in totality like logos, but specific passages or verses that God speaks and applies to specific situations in our lives. Dr. David Jeremiah continues on and says, *"The Bible is not the sword; the Bible is the armory filled with swords - filled with the sayings of God."* What an amazing visual...the Bible is packed with swords that are able to take down every lie, trick, and temptation the enemy throws our way.

This quote by Ray Stedman was too good not the share...listen to how he describes the work of the rhema in our lives. See if it reminds you of a time in your own life when God spoke to you:

"Sometimes when you are reading a passage of Scripture, the words seem suddenly to come alive. Take on flesh and bones, and leap off the page at you, or grow eyes that follow you everywhere you go, or develop a voice that echoes in your ears until you can't get away from it. This is the rhema of God, the sayings of God that strike home like arrows to the heart. This is the sword of the Spirit, which is the Word of God."

Keep in mind the sword of the Spirit is an offensive weapon. Jesus models exactly how to wield the sword against the enemy in Matthew 4:1-11. After 40 days in the wilderness without food, the devil arrived to tempt Jesus. The devil swung the temptation sword and Jesus swung back by quoting Scripture. Satan tried again, but this time his temptation was wrapped in Bible verses used out of context. Without skipping a beat, Jesus swung right back with, *"The Scriptures say..."* Satan didn't give up easily. One more time he swung tempting Jesus to take matters into His own hands and forgo God's plans. Impressively, Jesus came back with another powerful rhema response, *"The Scriptures say..."* The flawless, effortless quoting of scripture is extremely impressive. Oh, that we could aspire to be like Jesus!

Then, the devil went away, and angels came and cared for Jesus (Matthew 4:11). Don't scan over the last verse in this passage too quickly. You might miss some gold nuggets of truth. First, the enemy could not tolerate the spoken Word of God and he had to leave. James 4:7 says, *"Resist the devil, and he will flee from you."* By wielding the sword of the Spirit, you are in essence resisting the enemy. According to scripture, when we resist, he will flee! Second, as soon as the devil left, Jesus was cared for by God, and when we've stood strong offensively with our sword, He will come and minister to us too.

Do you want to respond to temptation the same way Jesus did? The arsenal of swords Jesus used came directly from the Bible and it's available to you too! **But you need to read it, memorize it and practice it.** You can't expect to go into battle and perform your best if you haven't developed your skills by digging into the Word. And if your adversary has prepared better than you...well, he's likely to have the upper hand in that battle.

To successfully take up the sword of the Spirit on the battlefield of trials, temptations and daily life, women need training. Between the Old and New Testament there are 66 books in the Bible, 1,189 chapters and 31,102 verses. Does all that knowledge and wisdom just transfer into our hearts and minds the day we first believe? No way! **It's our job, or rather our joy, to read, study, memorize, and put into practice God's Word.** William Gurnall said, *"A pilot without his chart, a scholar with his book and a soldier without his sword, are alike ridiculous. But, above all these, it is absurd for one to the think of being a Christian, without knowledge of the Word of God and some skill to use this weapon."*

By far, the absolute best training ground for learning to use "the Word as a weapon" is scripture memorization. Every verse committed to memory is like hiding a sword away in your heart. You might be worried that the scripture will get lost or misplaced inside your mind but you're not left to recall verses alone. God has given you a helper...the Holy Spirit who lives inside every believer. *"But the Helper, the Holy Spirit, whom the Father will send* *in my name, He will teach you all things and bring to your remembrance all that I have said to you"* (John 14:26 ESV). As we do our part to study and store God's Word in our hearts, we can rely on the Holy Spirit to teach us truth, to convince us of God's will and to help us remember all that we have learned.

Getting started on a scripture memory plan can seem overwhelming. Questions arise like, *Where do I start? How do I pick a verse to memorize? How do I find time? What if I am not skilled at memorizing?"* While these are all great questions, the best place to begin is just by beginning. **And that is what** *10 Verses to Know by Heart for Women* **is all about...it's a scripture memorization method to help women start committing the Bible to memory.** But it's more than mindless memorization; it's about chewing on, savoring and digesting verses so that they become part of you. This six step process, called the *Know by Heart Memory Method,* will help you memorize and internalize the most important words in your life – God's words.

Know by Heart Memory Method:

- **Step 1 – Pray. Write. Read.**
- **Step 2 – Examine the Verse**
- **Step 3 – Examine Before & After**
- **Step 4 – Examine Cross References**
- **Step 5 – Putting it All Together**
- **Step 6 – Personal Application**

Each of these six steps will lead you on a journey through your Bible to learn and understand the biblical context and biblical application of the Scripture (see page 8 for a description of each step). **It's important to note that the** *Know by Heart Memory Method* **is a strictly Bible-focused approach.** The best way to understand scripture is with scripture. So grab your Bible because you will need it! Just think when you complete this guided Scripture memory workbook you will have 10 swords in your arsenal and if you repeat this process, on your own with a new verse that you select once a week, after one year you will have memorized 52 new swords! Maybe the devil will think twice before coming after you. However, expect him to come because it's his singular goal to take down the Word of God. But with many swords in your heart and the Holy Spirit's help, on the battlefield of temptation, lies and deceit you'll discover new courage and new strength. And instead of cowering in fear or defeat you'll be standing in faith on the Word of God.

Sister, there is a full-on war in this world to confuse you about your true identity. The enemy doesn't want you to know who you are...he doesn't want you to reach your complete potential in Christ. In this *Know by Heart* memory workbook you are going to study and memorize 10 Scriptures that reveal your true identity according to God. You are going to fight the lies of the world with the truth of God! Get ready to discover your value and worth which is priceless.

This book can be done by yourself, in a group of women at church or in a small home group. Or, if you are a mom of a teen girl, you can study together with her! There is a version of this book available for teen girls called *10 Scripture to Know by Heart for Teen Girls!*

If you are a group facilitator who wants to lead a group, please reach out to me. I've been leading leading Bible study groups for several years and I'd love to share some helpful tips with you. You can contact me at *hello@jjgutierrezauthor.com.*

Supplies Needed for this Study:

- *10 Scripture to Know by Heart Women Workbook*
- **Bible**
- **Colored Pencils**
- **Pen or Pencil**
- **Scissors to Cut Out Index Cards**

"Your Word is a lamp to my feet and a light to my path."
Psalm 119:105

"I have hidden your Word in my heart that I might sin against you."
Psalm 119:11

"...and take up the sword of the Spirit, which is the Word of God."
Ephesians 6:17

Know by Heart Memory Method

Each chapter you'll begin with a short thought starter or a mini-devotional to get your mind centered on that week's topic. Next you'll see a set of Bible facts. Don't skim over this too quickly. Take note of the location of your Scripture, who wrote it and who was/is it written to. This will set the stage in your mind as you start the *Know by Heart* memory process.

The first five steps of the *Know by Heart* memory method are designed to focus solely on the Bible and what God says. Do your best to refrain from applying personal application until step six. It's important to listen first to God, then apply.

Prior to each step you'll rewrite the memory verse. Use this space to challenge yourself to try to write it without looking. On step four you are asked to write the verse using symbols or word pictures in place of important words (see step four for an example). You don't need to be an artist to complete this exercise. The practice of drawing uses an additional portion of your brain that helps to cement the verse into your memory.

Remember, the *Know by Heart Memory Method* **is not about mindless memorizing...it's about internalizing God's Word.**

STEP 1 -PRAY. WRITE. READ: Begin with prayer asking the Holy Spirit to empower you to learn and memorize that week's Scripture. Don't skip this necessary practice. You are not alone or left to your own strength and intellect. The Holy Spirit is your Helper. Then, you will write your *Know by Heart* memroy verse on an index card. There are cutout cards in the back of the book for your convenience. All memory verses are in the New Living Translation. After your index card is done, you will read three versions (New Living Translation, English Standard Version and Amplified Version) of the *Know by Heart* Bible verse and answer the questions that proceed.

STEP 2 - EXAMINE THE VERSE: The second step is to get up close to the verse and take note of specific words, actions and grammar. You will be prompted to underline, circle and draw arrows. Your verse might look like this:

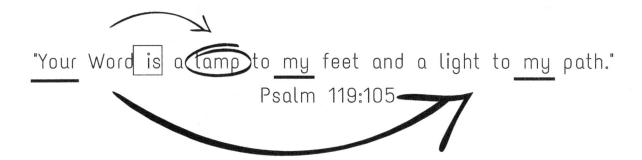

STEP 3 - EXAMINE THE BEFORE AND AFTER: In this section you'll be prompted to read verses before and after the *Know by Heart* memory verse. As you read them look for an overall theme, repeated words or any information that adds to understanding the context of the verse. The goal is to simply read what is written without adding or taking away. Answer the questions as prompted.

STEP 4 - EXAMINE THE CROSS REFERENCES: In this section you'll be prompted to rewrite the memory verse using symbols or word pictures in place of important words. See the example below. Also, you will explore cross reference Bible verses that are similar to and/or will add insight to the *Know by Heart* memory verse. Remember scripture explains scripture.

9

STEP 5 - PUTTING IT ALL TOGETHER: In this section you will look back over the the first four steps and bring all that you have learned together. Answer the questions as prompted. Specifically consider what insight you have gained about God.

STEP 6 - PERSONAL APPLICATION: This is the final step of the *Know by Heart* memory method process and very important to internalizing the verse. Take time to reflect upon each personal application question and respond. Finally, think of someone you can share this Scripture with...maybe a friend or family member who could benefit from knowing this Bible truth too.

Sister, I am so proud of you for taking time to learn and memorize God's Word. Are you ready to get started? Are you ready to store truth in your heart?

KNOW by HEART

Verse #1

Created

"So God created human beings in His own image. In the image of God He created them; male and female He created them." Genesis 1:27 NLT

Throughout the many stages of life, a woman's identity can experience one crisis after another. Whether it's trying to understand who you are at age twenty or age fifty, the question continually arises, *Who am I?* The enemy spreads lies and deceit. He wants women to believe the answer is found in success, independence, perfection or the ideal life. There's a strong temptation to buy into his lies or to listen to the world's distorted truth...a woman's identity resides in physical fitness, a beefed up bank account, a thriving career, a stellar education or harmonious relationships.

However, looking to anyone or anything other than God for answers about who you are will always leave you feeling empty. The truth is God never wonders who you are. Why? Because He created you! You are His...a woman whom God crafted and loves; a daughter of the King made in God's image, patterned after Him and in His likeness; different from all other creation because you were made to have a relationship with Him. In this week's *Know by Heart* memory verse you'll explore this marvelous truth - you are a beautiful creation of God's. And this truth has the power to bring every identity crisis to an end.

Know by Heart
Scripture #1

"So God created human beings in His own image. In the image of God He created them; male and female He created them." Genesis 1:27 NLT

Bible Verse Facts

BIBLE VERSE	Genesis 1:27
BOOK OF THE BIBLE	Genesis, Old Testament
GENRE	Historical Narrative
WRITTEN BY	Moses
WHO IS SPEAKING	Moses
INTENDED AUDIENCE	People of Israel
BACKGROUND	Genesis begins at the beginning of the world. Not only do we discover how the world came to be, but we also learn about ourselves. God created human beings on the sixth day of creation. Specifically He made them male and female. God blessed them and said, *"Be fruitful and multiply."* (Genesis 1:28) And He gave them authority and dominion over the earth and all the creatures within.

PRAY. WRITE. READ.

Pray   Ask the Holy Spirit to empower you to study, learn, understand and memorize this week's *Know By Heart* Scripture.

Write   Write this week's *Know by Heart* memory verse on an index card (*in the back of the book*).

Read   Read three versions: New Living Translation, English Standard Version and Amplified Version provided below.

"So God created human beings in His own image. In the image of God He created them; male and female He created them." Genesis 1:27 NLT

"So God created man in his own image, in the image of God he created him; male and female he created them." Genesis 1:27 ESV

"So God created man in His own image, in the image and likeness of God He created him; male and female He created them." Genesis 1:27 AMP

1. As you read the different versions, what stands out?

2. What questions does this Bible verse present to you? Write them below.

EXAMINE THE VERSE

Write this week's *Know by Heart* memory verse below.

[blank box]

Look at the questions below and follow the prompts to circle, box, underline and draw arrows on the *Know by Heart* verse below.

"So God created human beings in His own image. In the image of God He created them; male and female He created them." Genesis 1:27 NLT

1. Underline any pronouns - I, me, you, he, she, we, they, them, etc...

2. What words or phrases stand out to you? Circle them in the verse above.

3. Are there any connective words? Put a box around words like: and, but, or, so, therefore.

4. Are there any verbs or action words to take note of? Draw an arrow from the verb to the "what" of the action.

4. Pick two of the words you circled and look up the definitions in the dictionary. Write what you learned below.

1.

2.

5. Color this week's *Know by Heart* memory verse. Ponder the Scripture and ask the Holy Spirit to give you greater understanding. Use colored pencils or crayons only.

So GOD CREATED HUMAN BEINGS in His own *image*. IN THE IMAGE OF GOD HE created them; male & female He created them.

Genesis 1:27

Write this week's *Know by Heart* memory verse below.

Open your Bible and read the verses below. Answer the following questions.

1. Read Genesis 1:26. What appears or happens before the *Know by Heart* memory verse?

2. Read Genesis 1:28-31. What appears or happens after the *Know by Heart* memory verse?

3. Considering the passage what elements are found in the verses? Write the answers below.

   1. Who is speaking? Who was being spoken to?

   2. Is there a conflict, tension or sin being highlighted?

   3. Is there a stated purpose, instruction, command or promise given?

   4. Is anything being emphasized, repeated or compared to?

   5. Is there a connection between the *Know by Heart* memory verse and the before & after?

EXAMINE CROSS REFERENCES

Write this week's *Know by Heart* memory verse inserting word pictures or symbols in place of key words.

1. Read the following verses. What additional insight do they provide about God's creation of human beings?

   - Matthew 19:4

   - Mark 10:6

   - Genesis 5:1-2

2. What additional insight does Genesis 9:6 provide about the value God places on people who are made in His image?

3. Based on the verses above and Genesis 1:27, what truths do you learn about being a created human being?

PUTTING IT ALL TOGETHER

Write this week's *Know by Heart* memory verse by heart.

Now it's time to apply and reflect. Look over steps 1-4. Consider all you have read and learned and answer the following questions.

1. Turn back to the second question in Step One. Based on everything you have studied, are you able to answer any questions you wrote down? Write your answers here.

2. How would you summarize the meaning of Genesis 1:27?

3. What did you learn or discover about your identity according to God?

PERSONAL APPLICATION

Step Six

I am most tempted to question who I am when...

Remembering this *Know by Heart* memory verse will help me stand in my true identity because...

Actions I can take when I am feeling the culture, the world or the enemy trying to define who I am...

This Know by Heart memory verse strengthens my faith because...

Who can I share this Know by Heart memory verse with?

KNOW by HEART

Verse #2

Know by Heart
Women

Loved

"But God showed His great love for us by sending Christ to die for us while we were still sinners." Romans 5:8 NLT

Inside of every daughter of God is a desire to be loved. But love can be a confusing word due to the variety of ways we use it in our culture today. I love chocolate. I love the beach. I love my family. The constant use of this word dulls its value. When women hear or read, *"God loves you"* is that the same as loving a new car or going on vacation? No, not at all. It's not even close to the same kind of love.

The Bible says God loves you so much that He sent Jesus to die while you were still a sinner (Romans 5:8). Would you die for someone? Maybe...just maybe you'd be willing to die for a handful of people you love who love you back. But what about a rude grocery clerk, the man who just stole your grandma's purse or the co-worker spreading terrible rumors about you?

Let this truth soak in - God sent His Son to die for everyone! He sent His Son to die for you. Not because you are good or deserving...simply because He loves you. His love is a sacrificial kind of love and it's the love your heart craves. As you study and memorize this week's *Know by Heart* memory verse think about the value of God's sacrifice of love. It's a vastly different type of love than your desire for a box of chocolates!

22

Know by Heart

Scripture #2

"But God showed His great love for us by sending Christ to die for us while we were still sinners." Romans 5:8 NLT

Bible Verse Facts

BIBLE VERSE	Romans 5:8
BOOK OF THE BIBLE	Romans, New Testament
GENRE	Letter
WRITTEN BY	The Apostle Paul
WHO IS SPEAKING	Paul
INTENDED AUDIENCE	Christians in Rome & All Believers
BACKGROUND	Paul sent a letter ahead of his arrival in Rome to the Christian churches. His message reads more like a statement of faith rather than a typical letter. Paul reminds them, *all* are sinners in need of a Savior and one day God will judge sin. The law (though good) could not conquer sin...only Jesus's death on the cross and ressurection saves sinners.

PRAY. WRITE. READ.

Step One

Pray   Ask the Holy Spirit to empower you to study, learn, understand and memorize this week's *Know By Heart* Scripture.

Write   Write this week's *Know by Heart* memory verse on an index card (*in the back of the book*).

Read   Read three versions: New Living Translation, English Standard Version and Amplified Version provided below.

"But God showed His great love for us by sending Christ to die for us while we were still sinners." Romans 5:8 NLT

"But God shows his love for us in that while we were still sinners, Christ died for us." Romans 5:8 ESV

"But God shows and clearly proves His [own] love for us by the fact that while we were still sinners, Christ (the Messiah, the Anointed One) died for us." Romans 5:8 AMP

1. As you read the different versions, what stands out?

2. What questions does this Bible verse present to you? Write them below.

EXAMINE THE VERSE

Write this week's *Know by Heart* memory verse below.

Look at the questions below and follow the prompts to circle, box, underline and draw arrows on the *Know by Heart* verse below.

"But God showed His great love for us by sending Christ

to die for us while we were still sinners."

Romans 5:8 NLT

1. Underline any pronouns - I, me, you, he, she, we, they, them, etc...

2. What words or phrases stand out to you? Circle them in the verse above.

3. Are there any connective words? Put a box around words like: and, but, or, so, therefore.

4. Are there any verbs or action words to take note of? Draw an arrow from the verb to the "what" of the action.

4. Pick two of the words you circled and look up the definitions in the dictionary. Write what you learned below.

  1.

  2..

5. Color this week's *Know by Heart* memory verse. Ponder the Scripture and ask the Holy Spirit to give you greater understanding. Use colored pencils or crayons only.

But God showed His Great *love* for us by sending CHRIST TO DIE for us while we were still sinners.

Romans 5:8

Write this week's *Know by Heart* memory verse below.

Open your Bible and read the verses below. Answer the following questions.

1. Read Romans 5:6-7. What appears or happens before the *Know by Heart* memory verse?

2. Read Romans 5:9-11. What appears or happens after the *Know by Heart* memory verse?

3. Considering the passage what elements are found in the verses? Write the answers below.

   1. Who is speaking? Who was being spoken to?

   2. Is there a conflict, tension or sin being highlighted?

   3. Is there a stated purpose, instruction, command or promise given?

   4. Is anything being emphasized, repeated or compared to?

   5. Is there a connection between the *Know by Heart* memory verse and the before & after?

EXAMINE CROSS REFERENCES

Write this week's *Know by Heart* memory verse inserting word pictures or symbols in place of key words.

1. Read the following verses. What additional insight do they provide about God's love for you?

    *   John 3:16

    *   1 John 4:9-10

2. How does Ephesians 3:18 help you understand the depth of God's love for you?

Write this week's *Know by Heart* memory verse by heart.

Now it's time to apply and reflect. Look over steps 1-4. Consider all you have read and learned and answer the following questions.

1. Turn back to the second question on Step One. Based on everything you have studied, are you able to answer any questions you wrote down? Write your answers here.

2. How would you summarize the meaning of Romans 5:8?

3. What did you learn or discover about your identity according to God?

PERSONAL APPLICATION

Step Six

I am most tempted to feel unloved when...

Remembering this *Know by Heart* memory verse will help feel loved because...

Actions I can take when I am feeling unloved, disliked or unwanted...

This *Know by Heart* memory verse strengthens my faith because...

Who can I share this Know by Heart memory verse with?

KNOW by HEART

Verse #3

Known

"Oh LORD, you have examined my heart and you know everything about me."
Psalm 139:1 NLT

A common concern for many women is, *Does anybody really know me?* There are people who know about you...they know your name, what you look like, where you go to church & work, and maybe they know your favorite restaurant or what you did last week. Most likely your husband knows you best...your daily routine, where you keep your toothbrush and what your hopes and dreams are. Your best friend has inside knowledge of you too. She knows when you've had a bad day or when you've received the best news of your life. Your parents have known you from birth. They are well acquainted with your personality, weaknesses, strengths and many things about you. Yet, you can still feel like no one knows the real you...the inner part that is seldom revealed or shared with others - the secret thoughts and feelings (both good and bad) deep down in your heart.

However, the truth is you are known by God. He has intimate knowledge of you. Every unspoken thought, hidden emotion and unseen action He knows. Every tear you've cried, sin you've given into or temptation you've overcome He sees. He knows your motives, your hopes and dreams, your failures and weaknesses. Everything about you is noticed by Him and He loves you. As you study and memorize this week's *Know by Heart* memory verse think about how special and wonderful it is to be fully known by God.

"Oh LORD, you have examined my heart and you know everything about me." Psalm 139:1 NLT

Bible Verse Facts

BIBLE VERSE	Psalm 139:1
BOOK OF THE BIBLE	Psalms, Old Testament
GENRE	Poetry
WRITTEN BY	David
WHO IS SPEAKING	David
INTENDED AUDIENCE	People of Israel
BACKGROUND	The Psalms are a poetic expression of praise, worship and prayers to God. There are 150 Psalms and David wrote 73 of them including Psalm 139. In this specific Psalm, David praises and worships the all-knowing God who sees everything. God knows us and is with us. He is everywhere all the time.

PRAY. WRITE. READ.

Pray Ask the Holy Spirit to empower you to study, learn, understand and memorize this week's *Know By Heart* Scripture.

Write Write this week's *Know by Heart* memory verse on an index card (*in the back of the book*).

Read Read three versions: New Living Translation, English Standard Version and Amplified Version provided below.

"Oh LORD, you have examined my heart and you know everything about me." Psalm 139:1 NLT

"O Lord, you have searched me and known me!" Psalm 139:1 ESV

"Oh Lord, you have searched me [thoroughly] and have known me."
Psalm 139:1 AMP

1. As you read the different versions, what stands out?

2. What questions does this Bible verse present to you? Write them below.

Write this week's *Know by Heart* memory verse below.

Look at the questions below and follow the prompts to circle, box, underline and draw arrows on the *Know by Heart* verse below.

Oh LORD, you have examined my heart and you know

everything about me." Psalm 139:1 NLT

1. Underline any pronouns - I, me, you, he, she, we, they, them, etc...

2. What words or phrases stand out to you? Circle them in the verse above.

3. Are there any connective words? Put a box around words like: and, but, or, so, therefore.

4. Are there any verbs or action words to take note of? Draw an arrow from the verb to the "what" of the action.

4. Pick two of the words you circled and look up the definitions in the dictionary. Write what you learned below.

   1.

   2.

5. Color this week's *Know by Heart* memory verse. Ponder the Scripture and ask the Holy Spirit to give you greater understanding. Use colored pencils or crayons only.

Oh *LORD*, you have examined my *heart* and you know everything about me.

Psalm 139:1

Write this week's *Know by Heart* memory verse below.

Open your Bible and read Psalm 139:2-12. Answer the following questions.

1. What does God know about you? Write down 4 things David says God notices.

2. Where does God see you? Write down 5 places David mentions in the passage.

3. Considering the passage what elements are found in the verses? Write the answers below.

   1. Who is speaking? Who was being spoken to?

   2. Is there a conflict, tension or sin being highlighted?

   3. Is there a stated purpose, instruction, command or promise given?

   4. Is anything being emphasized, repeated or compared to?

   5. Is there a connection between the Know by Heart memory verse and the before & after?

EXAMINE CROSS REFERENCES

Write this week's *Know by Heart* memory verse inserting word pictures or symbols in place of key words.

1. Read the following verses. What additional insight do they provide about how *known* you are to God?

   • Psalm 44:21

   • Psalm 139:16

   • Psalm 56:8

   • Malachi 3:16

2. Based on these verses and Psalm 139:1, how much does God know you?

Write this week's *Know by Heart* memory verse by heart.

Now it's time to apply and reflect. Look over steps 1-4. Consider all you have read and learned and answer the following questions.

1. Turn back to the second question on step one. Based on everything you have studied are you able to answer any questions you wrote down? Write your answers here.

2. How would you summarize the meaning of Psalm 139:1?

3. What did you learn or discover about your identity according to God?

PERSONAL APPLICATION

Step Six

I am most tempted to feel like no one knows me when...

Remembering this *Know by Heart* memory verse will help me feel known by God because...

Actions I can take when I am feeling alone, unknown or unseen...

This *Know by Heart* memory verse strengthens my faith because...

Who can I share this Know by Heart memory verse with?

KNOW by HEART

Verse #4

Defined

"For we are God's masterpiece. He created us anew in Christ Jesus, so we can do the good works He planned for us long ago." Ephesians 2:10 NLT

The war to define a woman's identity is raging. The world, the culture and the enemy have launched a full attack to confuse and mislead daughters of God into believing lies about who they are. The goal is to undermine the truth found only in the Bible by degrading a woman's worth to a mere earthly experience. If the enemy can steer women to focus on me, me, me... what I want, what I think is right, what I desire, then her definition of who she is then becomes dramatically downgraded and the enemy wins.

But who has the right to define a woman? The enemy? The world or the culture? What about her Creator...does He possess the authority to define her? Think of an artist who has created a masterpiece. The artist is the expert in his craftsmanship. He has a purpose and plan for his creation and he retains the right to define his art. You are God's masterpiece. His workmanship. His creation. He alone is qualified to define you. As you study and memorize this week's *Know by Heart* memory verse turn away from noise of the world, the culture and the enemy, and turn to your Creator to define you. Listen to what God says about you, and be prepared because your identity just might strike gold!

"For we are God's masterpiece. He created us anew in Christ Jesus, so we can do the good works He planned for us long ago."
Ephesians 2:10 NLT

Bible Verse Facts

BIBLE VERSE	Ephesians 2:10
BOOK OF THE BIBLE	Ephesians, New Testament
GENRE	Letter
WRITTEN BY	The Apostle Paul
WHO IS SPEAKING	Paul
INTENDED AUDIENCE	Church in Ephesus & All Believers
BACKGROUND	Paul wrote to the church in Ephesus to strengthen their faith. An area of weakness is identity. Christians who don't know their identity in Christ are weakened and vulnerable for attack. Paul dedicated 12 verses in Ephesians to the true identity of Christians in Christ. (Ephesians 1:3, 1:4, 1:5-6, 1:7, 1:10-11, 1:13, 2:6, 2:10, 2:13, 3:6, 3:12, 5:29-30)

PRAY. WRITE. READ.

Step One

Pray Ask the Holy Spirit to empower you to study, learn, understand and memorize this week's *Know By Heart* Scripture.

Write Write this week's *Know by Heart* memory verse on an index card (*in the back of the book*).

Read Read three versions: New Living Translation, English Standard Version and Amplified Version provided below.

"For we are God's masterpiece. He created us anew in Christ Jesus, so we can do the good works He planned for us long ago." Ephesians 2:10 NLT

"For we are his workmanship, created in Christ Jesus for good works, which God prepared beforehand, that we should walk in them." Ephesians 2:10 ESV

"For we are God's [own] handiwork (His workmanship), recreated in Christ Jesus, [born anew] that we may do those good works which God predestined (planned beforehand) for us [taking paths which He prepared ahead of time}, that we should walk in them [living the good life which He prearranged and made ready for us to live.]" Ephesians 2:10 AMP

1. As you read the different versions, what stands out?

2. What questions does this Bible verse present to you? Write them below.

Write this week's *Know by Heart* memory verse below.

```

```

Look at the questions below and follow the prompts to circle, box, underline and draw arrows on the *Know by Heart* verse below.

"For we are God's masterpiece. He created us anew in

Christ Jesus, so we can do the good works He planned

for us long ago." Ephesians 2:10 NLT

1. Underline any pronouns - I, me, you, he, she, we, they, them, etc...

2. What words or phrases stand out to you? Circle them in the verse above.

3. Are there any connective words? Put a box around words like: and, but, or, so, therefore.

4. Are there any verbs or action words to take note of? Draw an arrow from the verb to the "what" of the action.

4. Pick two of the words you circled and look up the definitions in the dictionary. Write what you learned below.

   1.

   2.

5. Color this week's *Know by Heart* memory verse. Ponder the Scripture and ask the Holy Spirit to give you greater understanding. Use colored pencils or crayons only.

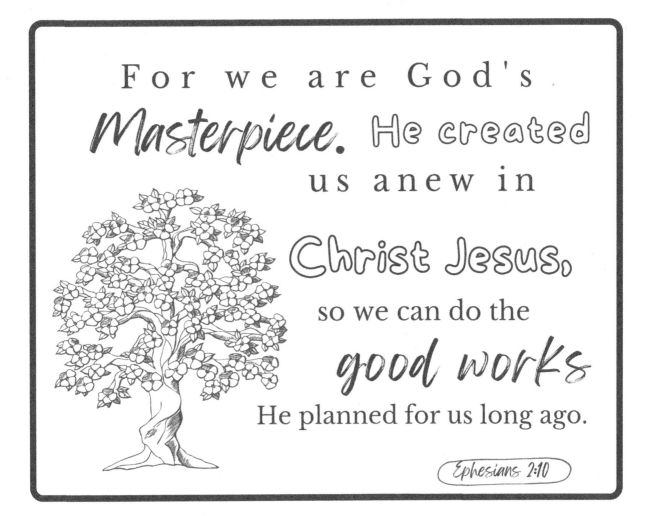

For we are God's Masterpiece. He created us anew in Christ Jesus, so we can do the good works He planned for us long ago.

Ephesians 2:10

Write this week's *Know by Heart* memory verse below.

Open your Bible and read the verses below. Answer the following questions.

1. Read Ephesians 2:1-9. What appears or happens before the *Know by Heart* memory verse?

3. Considering the passage what elements are found in the verses? Write the answers below.

1. Who is speaking? Who was being spoken to?

2. Is there a conflict, tension or sin being highlighted?

3. Did a miracle happen or was God's power highlighted?

4. Is there a stated purpose, instruction, command or promise given?

5. Is anything being emphasized, repeated or compared to?

Write this week's *Know by Heart* memory verse inserting word pictures or symbols in place of key words.

1. Read the following verses. What additional insight do they provide about the masterpiece God is creating in believers?

    - Psalm 100:3

    - Colossians 3:10

2. Based on Philippians 1:6, when will the masterpiece called *you* be completed?

3. According to Colossians 1:10 how should God's masterpieces live?

PUTTING IT ALL TOGETHER *Step Five*

Write this week's *Know by Heart* memory verse by heart.

Now it's time to apply and reflect. Look over steps 1-4. Consider all you have read and learned and answer the following questions.

1. Turn back to the second question on step one. Based on everything you have studied are you able to answer any questions you wrote down? Write your answers here.

2. How would you summarize the meaning of Ephesians 2:10?

3. What did you learn or discover about your identity according to God?

I am most tempted to feel defined by the world or the culture when...

Remembering this *Know by Heart* memory verse will help feel assured of who I am because...

Actions I can take when I am feeling insecure, unworthy, or of no value...

This *Know by Heart* memory verse strengthens my faith because...

Who can I share this Know by Heart memory verse with?

KNOW by HEART

Verse #5

Equipped

"For I can do everything through Christ, who gives me strength."
Philippians 4:13 NLT

Wife, mother, sister, friend...whatever your roles in life are it often feels like a tug-of-war between good days and hard days. When days are good life is pleasant, easy and carefree. But on hard days when life feels difficult, challenging and sometimes impossible you might wonder, *Can I manage this day, this task, this relationship, this problem?* Maybe you don't feel strong enough to withstand temptation or to follow God's way. Maybe the job ahead takes you out of your comfort zone and you don't believe you're capable or suitable. In these moments giving up appears to be the best option.

During times like these, when human ability isn't enough the answer is God's strength. God's equipped you with strength *in* and *through* Christ alone. Now God's strength isn't for everything you want to do...it's for everything God asks you to do. Things like being a kind wife, a caring and loving mom, a woman of integrity who is obedient to God even when it's hard or sharing your faith when you are afraid or it's inconvenient. As you study and memorize this week's *Know By Heart* Scripture ask God to infuse inner strength in you, through Christ, for everything He wants you to carry out.

Know
by Heart
Scripture #5

"For I can do everything through Christ, who gives me strength." Philippians 4:13 NLT

Bible Verse Facts

BIBLE VERSE	Philippians 4:13
BOOK OF THE BIBLE	Philippians, New Testament
GENRE	Letter
WRITTEN BY	The Apostle Paul
WHO IS SPEAKING	Paul
INTENDED AUDIENCE	Christians in Philippi & All Believers
BACKGROUND	More than anyone, Paul understood the need for strength beyond his own. It didn't matter if he possessed a lot or had nothing. Paul was equipped for every situation through strength in Christ and Christ alone. His words encourage believers to make Christ the center point of their lives and when they do, they will be equipped and strengthened.

PRAY. WRITE. READ.

Step One

Pray   Ask the Holy Spirit to empower you to study, learn, understand and memorize this week's *Know By Heart* Scripture.

Write   Write this week's *Know by Heart* memory verse on an index card (in the back of the book).

Read   Read three versions: New Living Translation, English Standard Version and Amplified Version provided below.

"For I can do everything through Christ, who gives me strength." Philippians 4:13

"I can do all things though Him who strengthens me." Philippians 4:13 ESV

"I have strength for all things in Christ Who empowers me [I am ready for anything and equal to anything through Him Who infuses inner strength into me; I am self-sufficient in Christ's sufficiency]." Philippians 4:13 AMP

1. As you read the different versions, what stands out?

2. What questions does this Bible verse present to you? Write them below.

Write this week's *Know by Heart* memory verse below.

Look at the questions below and follow the prompts to circle, box, underline and draw arrows on the *Know by Heart* verse below.

"For I can do everything through Christ, who gives me strength." Philippians 4:13

1. Underline any pronouns - I, me, you, he, she, we, they, them, etc...

2. What words or phrases stand out to you? Circle them in the verse above.

3. Are there any connective words? Put a box around words like: and, but, or, so, therefore.

4. Are there any verbs or action words to take note of? Draw an arrow from the verb to the "what" of the action.

4. Pick two of the words you circled and look up the definitions in the dictionary. Write what you learned below.

   1.

   2.

5. Color this week's *Know by Heart* memory verse. Ponder the Scripture and ask the Holy Spirit to give you greater understanding. Use colored pencils or crayons only.

FOR I CAN DO EVERYTHING

through Christ who gives me strength.

Philippians 4:13

Write this week's *Know by Heart* memory verse below.

Open your Bible and read Philippians 4:10-20. Answer the following questions.

1. Read Philippians 4:10-12. What appears or happens before the Know by Heart memory verse?

2. Read Philippians 4:14-20. What appears or happens after the Know by Heart memory verse?

3. Considering the entire passage answer the questions below.

   1. Who is speaking? Who was being spoken to?

   2. Is there a conflict, tension or sin being highlighted?

   3. Is there a stated purpose, instruction, command or promise given?

   4. Is anything being emphasized, repeated or compared to?

   5. Is there a connection between the Know by Heart memory verse and the before & after?

EXAMINE CROSS REFERENCES

Write this week's *Know by Heart* memory verse inserting word pictures or symbols in place of key words.

```

```

1. Read the following verses. What do you learn about how God equips you with strength? How can you experience God equipping you for all things?

   - 2 Corinthians 12:8-10

   - Isaiah 41:10

   - Ephesians 6:10

2. What additional insight does Isaiah 40:29-31 give you about *to whom* God gives strength?

3. Based on the verses above and Philippians 4:13 how are Christians equipped with God's strength in their lives?

PUTTING IT ALL TOGETHER

Write this week's *Know by Heart* memory verse by heart.

Now it's time to apply and reflect. Look over steps 1-4. Consider all you have read and learned and answer the following questions.

1. Turn back to the second question on step one. Based on everything you have studied are you able to answer any questions you wrote down? Write your answers here.

2. How would you summarize the meaning of Philippians 4:13?

3. What did you learn or discover about your identity according to God?

I am most tempted to feel like I can't when...

Remembering this *Know by Heart* memory verse will help feel equipped for all things because...

Actions I can take when I am feeling incapable, unqualified or weak...

This Know by Heart memory verse strengthens my faith because...

Who can I share this Know by Heart memory verse with?

KNOW by HEART

Verse #6

Gifted

"God has given each of you a gift from His great variety of spiritual gifts. Use them to serve one another." 1 Peter 4:10 NLT

Women can often find themselves in one of two camps. Camp one is filled with those who are aware of the talents and gifts God has given them. Many of these ladies believe their skills are for their own use. They get to decide how and when to use them. Camp two is filled with women who think they don't have any God-given abilities. This leaves these ladies feeling left out, not good enough or without purpose.

The truth is you are gifted! By God's gracious favor, He has bestowed a gift to everyone and that includes you. If you don't know your gifting, that is okay. Ask God to show you the gift He has placed within you. But be patient. It might take time before you discover it. However, whether you know your gifting or not, it's important to realize that your God-given abilities are not just for your own enjoyment...they are to be used to serve God and others. Be a faithful steward of your gifts because, by grace, God has entrusted them to you. As you study and memorize this week's *Know by Heart* Scripture ask God to reveal to you your gifts and to give you the desire to use them for His purposes.

Know by Heart
Scripture #6

"God has given each of you a gift from His great variety of spiritual gifts. Use them to serve one another." 1 Peter 4:10 NLT

Bible Verse Facts

BIBLE VERSE	I Peter 4:10
BOOK OF THE BIBLE	1 Peter, New Testament
GENRE	Letter
WRITTEN BY	Peter
WHO IS SPEAKING	Peter
INTENDED AUDIENCE	Scattered Jewish Christians & All Believers
BACKGROUND	I Peter is a letter of encouragement to Christians suffering for their faith. A reminder that suffering makes them partners with Christ who suffered for us. Peter comforts them with the hope of heaven and Christ's return. And he challenges believers to live holy lives in the midst of suffering. Jesus is the perfect example of faithful endurance under the pressure of suffering.

PRAY. WRITE. READ.

Pray   Ask the Holy Spirit to empower you to study, learn, understand and memorize this week's *Know By Heart* Scripture.

Write   Write this week's *Know by Heart* memory verse on an index card (*in the back of the book*).

Read   Read three versions: New Living Translation, English Standard Version and Amplified Version provided below.

"God has given each of you a gift from His great variety of spiritual gifts. Use them to serve one another." 1 Peter 4:10 NLT

"As each has received a gift, use it to serve one another, as good stewarts of varied grace." I Peter 4:10 ESV

"As each of you have received a gift (a particular spiritual talent, a gracious divine endowment), employ it for one another as [benefits] good trustees of God's many-sided grace [faithful stewards of the extremely diverse powers and gifts to Christians by unmerited favor]." I Peter 4:10 AMP

1. As you read the different versions, what stands out?

2. What questions does this Bible verse present to you? Write them below.

Write this week's *Know by Heart* memory verse below.

Look at the questions below and follow the prompts to circle, box, underline and draw arrows on the *Know by Heart* verse below.

"God has given each of you a gift from His great variety of spiritual gifts. Use them to serve one another." 1 Peter 4:10 NLT

1. Underline any pronouns - I, me, you, he, she, we, they, them, etc...

2. What words or phrases stand out to you? Circle them in the verse above.

3. Are there any connective words? Put a box around words like: and, but, or, so, therefore.

4. Are there any verbs or action words to take note of? Draw an arrow from the verb to the "what" of the action.

4. Pick two of the words you circled and look up the definitions in the dictionary. Write what you learned below.

     1.

     2.

5. Color this week's *Know by Heart* memory verse. Ponder the Scripture and ask the Holy Spirit to give you greater understanding. Use colored pencils or crayons only.

God has given each of you a GIFT from His great variety of spiritual gifts. Use them to SERVE one another.

I Peter 4:10

EXAMINE BEFORE & AFTER  Step Three

Write this week's *Know by Heart* memory verse below.

Open your Bible and read the verses below. Answer the following questions.

1. Read I Peter 4:1-9. What appears or happens before the *Know by Heart* memory verse?

2. Read I Peter 4:11-12. What appears or happens after the *Know by Heart* memory verse?

3. Considering the entire passage answer the questions below.

   1. Who is speaking? Who was being spoken to?

   2. Is there a conflict, tension or sin being highlighted?

   3. Is there a stated purpose, instruction, command or promise given?

   4. Is anything being emphasized, repeated or compared to?

   5. Is there a connection between the Know by Heart memory verse and the before & after?

Write this week's *Know by Heart* memory verse inserting word pictures or symbols in place of key words.

1. Read the following verse. What do you learn about who gives spiritual gifts? What are the gifts listed in this passage?

   • Romans 12:6-8

2. Read I Corinthians 12:7-11 and answer the questions below:

   • Who receives a gift?

   • What gifts are listed here?

   • Who decides what gift(s) a person receives?

3. Do you know what spiritual gift(s) God has given you? If you don't know that is okay. Pray and ask God to show you.

Write this week's *Know by Heart* memory verse by heart.

Now it's time to apply and reflect. Look over steps 1-4. Consider all you have read and learned and answer the following questions.

1. Turn back to the second question on step one. Based on everything you have studied are you able to answer any questions you wrote down? Write your answers here.

2. How would you summarize the meaning of 1 Peter 4:10?

3. What did you learn or discover about your identity according to God?

Step Six

I am most tempted to feel like God didn't give me a spiritual gift when...

Remembering this *Know by Heart* memory verse will help me feel my life has purpose because...

Actions I can take when I am feeling untalented, useless, or purposeless...

This *Know by Heart* memory verse strengthens my faith because...

Who can I share this Know by Heart memory verse with?

KNOW by HEART

Verse #7

Hope Filled

"For I know the plans I have for you," says the LORD. "They are plans for good and not for disaster, to give you a future and a hope." Jeremiah 29:11 NLT

Grown women are not immune from the feelings of hopelessness. Life is hard, and at times, the future can look blurry. Maybe it's moving to a new city, an ill spouse or child, a broken relationship or the pressures of temptation causing the feelings of helplessness or depression. Maybe it's feeling stuck in a situation thinking there is no way out. During the toughest of times hope is needed the most. Yet, it's in suffering, hardship and pain that hope seems the furthest away.

Jeremiah was called by God to deliver a message to a hopeless nation. God's people were exiled and living among a pagan culture. They might have felt abandoned or forgotten by God. Jeremiah encouraged them with a promise from God – He had a plan for their lives, a future that included good not harm. Though their captivity would last 70 years, God would restore them. In the middle of their suffering God gave them hope for the future. As you study and memorize this week's *Know by Heart* Scripture recognize that God has filled you with hope for the future. Maybe you need to consider where your hope is stemming from...is it the visible world or our invisible God?

Know by Heart
Scripture #7

"For I know the plans I have for you,' says the LORD. 'They are plans for good and not for disaster, to give you a future and a hope."
Jeremiah 29:11 NLT

Bible Verse Facts

BIBLE VERSE	Jeremiah 29:11
BOOK OF THE BIBLE	Jeremiah, Old Testament
GENRE	Major Prophet
WRITTEN BY	Jeremiah
WHO IS SPEAKING	The Lord
INTENDED AUDIENCE	Judah, Capital City of Jerusalem
BACKGROUND	God's people were in exile, living in a pagan land. After 70 years of captivity God promised to restore them. God knew their future and His plan for their lives, good plans filled with hope. However, God's blessing wasn't reserved just for the future. It would abound in the midst of their captivity if they would seek Him with all their hearts.

PRAY. WRITE. READ.

Step One

Pray Ask the Holy Spirit to empower you to study, learn, understand and memorize this week's *Know By Heart* Scripture.

Write Write this week's *Know by Heart* memory verse on an index card (i*n the back of the book*).

Read Read three versions: New Living Translation, English Standard Version and Amplified Version provided below.

"For I know the plans I have for you,' says the LORD. 'They are plans for good and not for disaster, to give you a future and a hope." Jeremiah 29:11 NLT

"For I know the plans I have for you, declares the LORD, plans for welfare and not for evil, to give you a future and a hope." Jeremiah 29:11 ESV

"For I know the thoughts and plans that I have for you, says the Lord, thoughts and plans for welfare and peace and not for evil, to give you hope in your final outcome." Jeremiah 29:11 AMP

1. As you read the different versions, what stands out?

2. What questions does this Bible verse present to you? Write them below.

EXAMINE THE VERSE

Step Two

Write this week's *Know by Heart* memory verse below.

Look at the questions below and follow the prompts to circle, box, underline and draw arrows on the *Know by Heart* verse below.

"For I know the plans I have for you,' says the LORD. 'They are plans for good and not for disaster, to give you a future and a hope." Jeremiah 29:11 NLT

1. Underline any pronouns - I, me, you, he, she, we, they, them, etc...

2. What words or phrases stand out to you? Circle them in the verse above.

3. Are there any connective words? Put a box around words like: and, but, or, so, therefore.

4. Are there any verbs or action words to take note of? Draw an arrow from the verb to the "what" of the action.

4. Pick two of the words you circled and look up the definitions in the dictionary. Write what you learned below.

1.

2.

5. Color this week's *Know by Heart* memory verse. Ponder the Scripture and ask the Holy Spirit to give you greater understanding. Use colored pencils or crayons only.

"For I know the *plans* I have for you," says the Lord. "They are *plans* for GOOD not for disaster, to give you a FUTURE AND HOPE."

Jeremiah 29:11

EXAMINE BEFORE & AFTER

Write this week's *Know by Heart* memory verse below.

Open your Bible and read the verses below. Answer the following questions.

1. Read Jeremiah 29:4-10. What appears or happens before the *Know by Heart* memory verse?

2. Read Jeremiah 29:12-14. What appears or happens after the *Know by Heart* memory verse?

3. Considering the entire passage answer the questions below.

1. Who is speaking? Who was being spoken to?

2. Is there a conflict, tension or sin being highlighted?

3. Is there a stated purpose, instruction, command or promise given?

4. Is anything being emphasized, repeated or compared to?

5. Is there a connection between the Know by Heart memory verse and the before & after?

EXAMINE CROSS REFERENCES

Write this week's *Know by Heart* memory verse inserting word pictures or symbols in place of key words.

1. Read the following verses. What do you learn about hope? How can you experience the hope of God amidst any circumstance?

   - Psalm 40:5

   - Isaiah 40:9-11

2. What additional insight does Isaiah 55:8-12 give you about having hope in hard times?

3. Based on the verses above and Jeremiah 29:11 what anchors your hope during trials, hardships and challenges?

Write this week's *Know by Heart* memory verse by heart.

Now it's time to apply and reflect. Look over steps 1-4. Consider all you have read and learned and answer the following questions.

1. Turn back to the second question on step one. Based on everything you have studied are you able to answer any questions you wrote down? Write your answers here.

2. How would you summarize the meaning of Jeremiah 29:11?

3. What did you learn or discover about your identity according to God?

I am most tempted to lose hope when...

Remembering this Know by Heart memory verse will help restore my hope in hard times because...

Actions I can take when I am feeling hopeless, downcast or depressed...

This Know by Heart memory verse strengthens my faith because...

Who can I share this Know by Heart memory verse with?

KNOW by HEART

Verse #8

Forgiven

"But if we confess our sins to Him, He is faithful and just to forgive us our sins and cleanse us from all wickedness." I John 1:9 NLT

At times, a daughter of God might feel her sin is unforgiveable, and instead of confessing it, she hides it. The secret becomes a heavy burden of shame and guilt that causes her to bury it deep inside her heart. Other times, she may think, *I don't sin or my sin is minor...little tiny things that don't hurt anyone.* This kind of thinking puffs up her pride (pride is sin) while causing unwanted distance between her and God.

Sin is just a fancy word for disobeying God. Everyone has sinned. I'll prove it to you...have you ever lied, gossiped, complained or gone over the speed limit? Yep, you are a sinner. But sometimes women can find themselves doing unimaginable things against God's plan for their lives too. It doesn't matter the type or weight of sin, what matters is through Jesus Christ forgiveness is possible. The path to forgiveness is confession. Confession is like cleaning your house...it wipes out all the dirt. When you confess your sins to God, He is faithful to wash away your guilt and shame and to forgive you. As you study and memorize this week's *Know by Heart* Scripture humbly confess your sins to God and receive His forgiveness.

Know by Heart
Scripture #8

"But if we confess our sins to Him, He is faithful and just to forgive us our sins and cleanse us from all wickedness." I John 1:9 NLT

Bible Verse Facts

BIBLE VERSE	1 John 1:9
BOOK OF THE BIBLE	1 John, New Testament
GENRE	Letter
WRITTEN BY	The Apostle John
WHO IS SPEAKING	John
INTENDED AUDIENCE	Gentile Churches & All Believers
BACKGROUND	The apostle John authored five books in the New Testament. 1 John was written to Christians facing persecution and false teaching. Some believers were conforming to the culture's standards and thus compromising their faith. John encouraged Christians to live in the Light, the truth of Jesus, and to love God and each other.

PRAY. WRITE. READ.

Pray Ask the Holy Spirit to empower you to study, learn, understand and memorize this week's *Know By Heart* Scripture.

Write Write this week's *Know by Heart* memory verse on an index card (*in the back of the book*).

Read Read three versions: New Living Translation, English Standard Version and Amplified Version provided below.

"But if we confess our sins to Him, He is faithful and just to forgive us our sins and cleanse us from all wickedness." I John 1:9 NLT

"If we confess our sins, he is faithful and just to forgive us our sins and to cleanse us from all unrighteousness." 1 John 1:9 ESV

"If we [freely] admit that we have sinned and confess our sins, He is faithful and just (true to His own nature and promises) and will forgive our sins [dismiss our lawlessness] and [continuously] cleanse us from all our unrighteousness [everything not in conformity to His will in purpose, thought, and action]." 1 John 1:9 AMP

1. As you read the different versions, what stands out?

2. What questions does this Bible verse present to you? Write them below.

EXAMINE THE VERSE

Step Two

Write this week's *Know by Heart* memory verse below.

Look at the questions below and follow the prompts to circle, box, underline and draw arrows on the *Know by Heart* verse below.

"But if we confess our sins to Him, He is faithful and just to forgive us our sins and cleanse us from all wickedness." I John 1:9 NLT

1. Underline any pronouns - I, me, you, he, she, we, they, them, etc...

2. What words or phrases stand out to you? Circle them in the verse above.

3. Are there any connective words? Put a box around words like: and, but, or, so, therefore.

4. Are there any verbs or action words to take note of? Draw an arrow from the verb to the "what" of the action.

4. Pick two of the words you circled and look up the definitions in the dictionary. Write what you learned below.

    1.

    2.

5. Color this week's *Know by Heart* memory verse. Ponder the Scripture and ask the Holy Spirit to give you greater understanding. Use colored pencils or crayons only.

But if we CONFESS OUR SINS TO HIM, HE IS faithful & just to FORGIVE US our sins and to cleanse us from all wickedness.

1 John 1:9

Write this week's *Know by Heart* memory verse below.

> [blank box]

Open your Bible and read the verses below. Answer the following questions.

1. Read 1 John 1:5-8. What appears or happens before the *Know by Heart* memory verse?

2. Read 1 John 1:10 What appears or happens after the *Know by Heart* memory verse?

3. Considering the entire passage answer the questions below.

   1. Who is speaking? Who was being spoken to?

   2. Is there a conflict, tension or sin being highlighted?

   3. Is there a stated purpose, instruction, command or promise given?

   4. Is anything being emphasized, repeated or compared to?

   5. Is there a connection between the *Know by Heart* memory verse and the before & after?

EXAMINE CROSS REFERENCES

Write this week's *Know by Heart* memory verse inserting word pictures or symbols in place of key words.

1. Read the following verses. What do you learn about God's forgiveness? How can you experience the forgiveness of your sins ?

    • Psalm 32:5

    • Proverbs 28:13

2. What additional insight does Hebrews 9:14 provide about forgiveness? Who is the perfect sacrifice on your behalf?

3. Based on the verses above and 1 John 1:9 what is your part in receiving forgiveness and what part can only Christ do you for?

Write this week's *Know by Heart* memory verse by heart.

Now it's time to apply and reflect. Look over steps 1-4. Consider all you have read and learned and answer the following questions.

1. Turn back to the second question on step one. Based on everything you have studied are you able to answer any questions you wrote down? Write your answers here.

2. How would you summarize the meaning of 1 John 1:9?

3. What did you learn or discover about your identity according to God?

PERSONAL APPLICATION

I am most tempted to feel like God's forgiveness won't cover my sins when...

Remembering this *Know by Heart* memory verse will help me to receive God's forgiveness because...

Actions I can take when I am feeling guilty, convicted, or remorseful...

This *Know by Heart* memory verse strengthens my faith because...

Who can I share this Know by Heart memory verse with?

KNOW by HEART

Verse #9

Cared For

"The LORD is my shepherd; I have everything I need." Psalm 23:1 NLT

Women flourish when they feel loved and cared for. There's comfort in knowing someone is looking out for and tending to her needs. Whether it's her husband looking out for her daily needs, a friend caring about her well-being, a boss helping her excel or a pastor overseeing her spiritual growth... when someone shows an interest in her, she feels cared for.

In the Bible, David compared his relationship with God to a sheep a with shepherd. A shepherd cares for his sheep by providing, protecting, comforting and leading his flock. The sheep need not worry or fear for the shepherd meets all their needs. Feeling cared for is the result of staying close to and following the shepherd. You can have the same relationship with God. He is your Shepherd. You are cared for. However, the challenge is your desire for independence. The more self-reliant you become the easier it is to walk away from the Shepherd...the only One who can meet all your needs. As you study and memorize this week's *Know by Heart* Scripture ask yourself, *Is the LORD my Shepherd? Am I following close behind Him, relying on Him to meet my deepest needs?*

Know
by Heart
Scripture #9

"The LORD is my shepherd; I have everything I need." Psalm 23:1 NLT

Bible Verse Facts

BIBLE VERSE	Psalm 23:1
BOOK OF THE BIBLE	Psalm, Old Testament
GENRE	Poetry
WRITTEN BY	David
WHO IS SPEAKING	David
INTENDED AUDIENCE	People of Israel
BACKGROUND	David describes his personal relationship with God as a sheep is to his shepherd. No one knows David's age when he wrote this Psalm. However, as a shepherd boy he knew first-hand what it meant to feed, guide and protect sheep. It's possible in David's later years as king he looked back over his life and recognized the hand of God sustaining him by feeding, guiding and protecting him.

PRAY. WRITE. READ.

Step One

Pray — Ask the Holy Spirit to empower you to study, learn, understand and memorize this week's *Know By Heart* Scripture.

Write — Write this week's *Know by Heart* memory verse on an index card (in the back of the book).

Read — Read three versions: New Living Translation, English Standard Version and Amplified Version provided below.

"The LORD is my shepherd; I have everything I need." Psalm 23:1 NLT

"The LORD is my shepherd; I shall not want." Psalm 23:1 ESV

"The Lord is my Shepherd [to feed, guide, and shield me], I shall not lack." Psalm 23:1 AMP

1. As you read the different versions, what stands out?

2. What questions does this Bible verse present to you? Write them below.

Write this week's *Know by Heart* memory verse below.

[ ]

Look at the questions below and follow the prompts to circle, box, underline and draw arrows on the *Know by Heart* verse below.

The LORD is my shepherd; I have everything I need."

Psalm 23:1 NLT

1. Underline any pronouns - I, me, you, he, she, we, they, them, etc...

2. What words or phrases stand out to you? Circle them in the verse above.

3. Are there any connective words? Put a box around words like: and, but, or, so, therefore.

4. Are there any verbs or action words to take note of? Draw an arrow from the verb to the "what" of the action.

4. Pick two of the words you circled and look up the definitions in the dictionary. Write what you learned below.

    1.

    2.

5. Color this week's *Know by Heart* memory verse. Ponder the Scripture and ask the Holy Spirit to give you greater understanding. Use colored pencils or crayons only.

THE LORD IS My SHEPHERD
I HAVE EVERYTHING I NEED.

Psalm 23:1

Write this week's *Know by Heart* memory verse below.

1. Open your Bible to Psalm 23. Read the verses below and fill out the chart. Consider: How is God a shepherd to His sheep? What needs is He meeting?

Verse	Needs of the Sheep	How God Meets those Needs
Psalm 23:1		
Psalm 23:2		
Psalm 23:3		
Psalm 23:4		
Psalm 23:5		
Psalm 23:6		

2. Is there a connection between the *Know by Heart* memory verse and the verses after?

Write this week's *Know by Heart* memory verse inserting word pictures or symbols in place of key words.

┌───┐
│   │
│   │
│   │
│   │
│   │
└───┘

1. Read the following verses. What do you learn about the LORD as your Shepherd?

- John 10:11

- I Peter 2:25

- Isaiah 40:11

- Ezekiel 34:11-16

2. Read the following verses. What do you learn about the Shepherd's care and provision for His sheep?

- Philippians 4:19

- 2 Corinthians 9:8

Write this week's *Know by Heart* memory verse by heart.

Now it's time to apply and reflect. Look over steps 1-4. Consider all you have read and learned and answer the following questions.

1. Turn back to the second question on step one. Based on everything you have studied are you able to answer any questions you wrote down? Write your answers here.

2. How would you summarize the meaning of Psalm 23:1?

3. What did you learn or discover about your identity according to God?

PERSONAL APPLICATION

I am most tempted to feel uncared for when...

Remembering this *Know by Heart* memory verse will help me feel tended after, nurtured and protected for because...

Actions I can take when I am feeling like nobody cares about me...

This *Know by Heart* memory verse strengthens my faith because...

Who can I share this Know by Heart memory verse with?

KNOW by HEART

Verse #10

Blessed

"All praise to God, the Father of our Lord Jesus Christ, who has blessed us with every spiritual blessing in the heavenly realms because we are united with Christ."
Ephesians 1:3 NLT

Sister in Christ, as we reach the last *Know by Heart* memory verse let's recap your true identity according to God: you are created, loved, known, defined by God, equipped, gifted, hope filled, forgiven and cared for.

What does all this mean?

You are one blessed lady!

But it gets better...God has blessed you, in Christ, to have a relationship with Him. You can enjoy all the spiritual blessings of God right here, right now because you belong to Christ. As you study and memorize this week's *Know by Heart* Scripture don't take for granted the blessings God has bestowed upon you. These blessings weren't earned by you or anyone else. They are free gifts from God because you are a child of God and He loves you so very much!

Know by Heart

Scripture #10

Bible Verse Facts

BIBLE VERSE	Ephesians 1:3
BOOK OF THE BIBLE	Ephesians, New Testament
GENRE	Letter
WRITTEN BY	The Apostle Paul
WHO IS SPEAKING	Paul
INTENDED AUDIENCE	Church in Ephesus & All Believers
BACKGROUND	As with all of Paul's letters he begins by stating the letter is from him and to whom it is addressed. Then, Paul gives a short warm greeting followed by a reminder that *in* Christ believers have been showered with spiritual blessings and God's kindness. Christians can know God, receive salvation & forgiveness for sins and have the hope of eternity in heaven.

PRAY. WRITE. READ.

Step One

Pray   Ask the Holy Spirit to empower you to study, learn, understand and memorize this week's *Know By Heart* Scripture.

Write   Write this week's *Know by Heart* memory verse on an index card (i*n the back of the book*).

Read   Read three versions: New Living Translation, English Standard Version and Amplified Version provided below.

"All praise to God, the Father of our Lord Jesus Christ, who has blessed us with every spiritual blessing in the heavenly realms because we are united with Christ." Ephesians 1:3 NLT

"Blessed be the God and Father of our Lord Jesus Christ, who has blessed us in Christ with every spiritual blessing in the heavenly places." Ephesians 1:3 ESV

"May blessings (praise, laudation, and eulogy) be to the God of our Lord Jesus Christ (the Messiah) Who has blessed us in Christ with every spiritual (given by the Holy Spirit) blessing in the heavenly realm!" Ephesians 1:3 AMP

1. As you read the different versions, what stands out?

2. What questions does this Bible verse present to you? Write them below.

Write this week's *Know by Heart* memory verse below.

Look at the questions below and follow the prompts to circle, box, underline and draw arrows on the *Know by Heart* verse below.

"All praise to God, the Father of our Lord Jesus Christ,

who has blessed us with every spiritual blessing in the

heavenly realms because we are united with Christ."

Ephesians 1:3 NLT

1. Underline any pronouns - I, me, you, he, she, we, they, them, etc...

2. What words or phrases stand out to you? Circle them in the verse above.

3. Are there any connective words? Put a box around words like: and, but, or, so, therefore.

4. Are there any verbs or action words to take note of? Draw an arrow from the verb to the "what" of the action.

4. Pick two of the words you circled and look up the definitions in the dictionary. Write what you learned below.

    1.

    2.

5. Color this week's *Know by Heart* memory verse. Ponder the Scripture and ask the Holy Spirit to give you greater understanding. Use colored pencils or crayons only.

All praise to God, the Father of our *Lord Jesus Christ,* who has blessed us with every spiritual blessing in the heavenly realms because we are united with Christ.

Ephesians 1:3

EXAMINE BEFORE & AFTER

Step Three

Write this week's *Know by Heart* memory verse below.

Open your Bible and read the verses below. Answer the following questions.

1. Read Ephesians 1:1-2. What appears or happens before the *Know by Heart* memory verse?

2. Read Ephesians 1:4-8. What appears or happens after the *Know by Heart* memory verse?

3. Considering the entire passage answer the questions below.

1. Who is speaking? Who was being spoken to?

2. Is there a conflict, tension or sin being highlighted?

3. Is there a stated purpose, instruction, command or promise given?

4. Is anything being emphasized, repeated or compared to?

5. Is there a connection between the *Know by Heart* memory verse and the before & after?

EXAMINE CROSS REFERENCES

Write this week's *Know by Heart* memory verse inserting word pictures or symbols in place of key words.

1. Read the following verses. What do you learn about God's blessings? Who do the blessings flow from?

   - 2 Corinthians 1:3

   - 1 Peter 1:3

2. Based on the verses above and Ephesians 1:3 how are Christians blessed with every spiritual blessing?

Write this week's *Know by Heart* memory verse by heart.

Now it's time to apply and reflect. Look over steps 1-4. Consider all you have read and learned and answer the following questions.

1. Turn back to the second question on step one. Based on everything you have studied are you able to answer any questions you wrote down? Write your answers here.

2. How would you summarize the meaning of Ephesians 1:3?

3. What did you learn or discover about your identity according to God?

I am most tempted to feel like I'm not blessed when...

Remembering this *Know by Heart* memory verse will help feel God's favor because...

141

Actions I can take when I am feeling unhappy, lousy or that everything is going wrong...

This *Know by Heart* memory verse strengthens my faith because...

Who can I share this Know by Heart memory verse with?

KNOW by HEART

Blank Worksheet

Pick Your Own

Repeat the *Know by Heart Memory Method* on your own with any Bible verse. Simply select a verse and use this blank worksheet to lead you step by step through the process of memorizing and internalizing God's Word.

Know
by Heart
Blank Template

Write your verse here & fill in the blanks below:

Bible Verse Facts

This information can often be found in the introduction section of the book your verse is found in.

BIBLE VERSE

BOOK OF THE BIBLE

GENRE

WRITTEN BY

WHO IS SPEAKING

INTENDED AUDIENCE

BACKGROUND

PRAY. WRITE. READ.

Pray   Ask the Holy Spirit to empower you to study, learn, understand and memorize this week's *Know By Heart* Scripture.

Write   Write your *Know by Heart* memory verse on an index card (*in the back of the book*).

Read   Read three versions: New Living Translation, English Standard Version and Amplified Version provided below.

NLT:

ESV:

AMP:

1. As you read the different versions, what stands out?

2. What questions does this Bible verse present to you? Write them below.

EXAMINE THE VERSE

Write this week's *Know by Heart* memory verse below.

[ ]

Write your *Know by Heart* verse below and look at the questions below and follow the prompts to circle, box, underline and draw arrows.

1. Underline any pronouns - I, me, you, he, she, we, they, them, etc...

2. What words or phrases stand out to you? Circle them in the verse above.

3. Are there any connective words? Put a box around words like: and, but, or, so, therefore.

4. Are there any verbs or action words to take note of? Draw an arrow from the verb to the "what" of the action.

4. Pick two of the words you circled and look up the definitions in the dictionary. Write what you learned below.

    1.

    2.

5. Draw a picture of your *Know by Heart* memory verse. Ponder the Scripture & ask the Holy Spirit to give you greater understanding. Use colored pencils or crayons only.

Write this week's *Know by Heart* memory verse below.

```
[blank box]
```

Open your Bible and read the verses before and after as it makes sense. Answer the following questions.

1. Read 2-5 verses before. What appears or happens before the *Know by Heart* memory verse?

2. Read 2-5 verses after. What appears or happens after the *Know by Heart* memory verse?

3. Considering the entire passage answer the questions below.

   1. Who is speaking? Who was being spoken to?

   2. Is there a conflict, tension or sin being highlighted?

   3. Is there a stated purpose, instruction, command or promise given?

   4. Is anything being emphasized, repeated or compared to?

   5. Is there a connection between the Know by Heart memory verse and the before & after?

EXAMINE CROSS REFERENCES

Write this week's *Know by Heart* memory verse inserting word pictures or symbols in place of key words.

1. Look in a study Bible for cross references. Write them below. Ask for help if needed. Try to find 2 cross reference verses.

  •

  •

2. What additional insight do the cross referecnces provide you?

Write this week's *Know by Heart* memory verse by heart.

Now it's time to apply and reflect. Look over steps 1-4. Consider all you have read and learned and answer the following questions.

1. Turn back to the second question on step one. Based on everything you have studied are you able to answer any questions you wrote down? Write your answers here.

2. How would you summarize the meaning of your verse?

3. What did you learn or discover about your identity according to God, God's character or His Word?

PERSONAL APPLICATION

I am most tempted to forget this verse when...

Remembering this *Know by Heart* memory verse will help me because...

Actions I can take when my feelings don't line up with this truth...

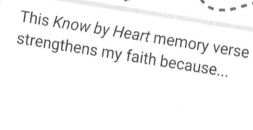

This *Know by Heart* memory verse strengthens my faith because...

Who can I share this Know by Heart memory verse with?

KNOW ❤ by HEART

Cut out index cards to write your *Know by Heart* memory Scripture on each week. Place your card in a location that will be seen every day...your bathroom mirror, desk or refrigerator. This practice will help you keep the verse at the top of your mind.

Know by Heart Memory Verse

Know by Heart Memory Verse

Know by Heart Memory Verse

Intentionally Left Blank

Know by Heart Memory Verse

Know by Heart Memory Verse

Know by Heart Memory Verse

Intentionally Left Blank

Know by Heart Memory Verse

Know by Heart Memory Verse

Know by Heart Memory Verse

Intentionally Left Blank

Know by Heart Memory Verse

Know by Heart Memory Verse

Know by Heart Memory Verse

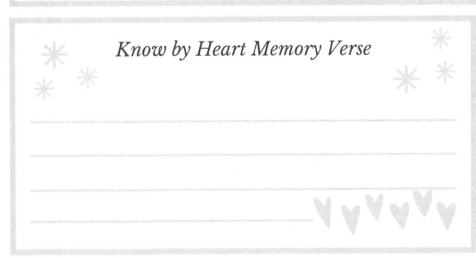

Intentionally Left Blank

Book Sites

Introduction

Chuck Swindoll, Growing Strong in the Seasons of Life. Zondervan, 1983, 61.

Alistair Begg. "Sword of the Spirit Part 1." Truth for Life Daily Program with Alistair Begg, July 1, 2021, *https://podcasts.apple.com/us/podcast/truth-for-life-daily-program/id91473880?i=1000525700020*

D Dr. David Jeremiah. Overcomer. W Publishing, an imprint of Thomas Nelson, 2018, 147.

Ray C. Steadman, Spiritual Warfare: Winning the Daily Battle with Satan. (Portland, OR: Multnomah Press 1975) 116.

William Gurnall. The Christian in Complete Armor, 3 Volume set. (remaining info unknown).

Facilitating a Know by Heart Group

I am sure you have heard your pastor say more than once, "join a group" and that's because within groups our learning and growing potential expands. Together we feel known, heard and accepted, and we gain valuable new insights from each other.

Gathering a group of women who want to grow closer to God while experiencing connection and support takes a step of faith. By starting your own small group you are opening a space where women can experience community while deepening their relationship with the Lord.

How do I start a *Know by Heart* Small Group?

If you feel a nudge in your heart to start a *Know by Heart* small group begin by praying. God might already be prompting your heart, but it's always wise to check in with Him first. Then, when you are ready to proceed, follow these steps:

- Gather a group of women. It could be ladies from church, your next door neighbors, or if you are a mom of a teen girl, you could invite other moms with teen girls. For the a mom and teen girls group, the girls would need a copy of *10 Scriptures to Know by Heart for Teen Girls*. If you need help, reach out at *hello@jjgutierrezauthor.com*. I would love to offer support, guidance and encouragement along the way.
- Pick a start date, day of the week, time and location. Keep in mind you will need 11 weeks to complete the study: Opening week and 10 weeks for each chapter.

- Call or send an email and invite any ladies you think might be interested at least 2-3 weeks in advance.
- All participants, including the leaders need:
  - The book: *10 Scriptures to Know by Heart for Women*
  - A physical Bible
  - Colored pencils
  - A dictionary or dictionary app

What makes a good facilitator?

A facilitator is simply a person who is willing to lead the discussion about each chapter. They aid in the process of helping participants learn from their own experiences and shared information. A good facilitator will follow a few simple guidelines:

- Respecting the time of the group by starting and ending on time
- Giving everyone in the group an equal opportunity to share
- Not allowing the discussion to become advice giving or counseling
- Staying away from giving your opinion about some else's situation
- Creating a safe and trusted environment where women can share honestly
- Staying focused on the intended discussion and lesson
- Adding fun ice breakers to the beginning of each meeting
- Celebrating at the end with a potluck

I am excited you are considering starting a *Know by Heart* small group! It's been my experience whenever I step out in faith to lead a group God reveals Himself to me in new and amazing ways, and I am confident you will experience that too. But also beware that the enemy may try to attack you with fear or second guessing your ability to lead. He certainly doesn't want women helping other women grow closer to God by digging into His Word. Instead of becoming discouraged, consider it confirmation that you are courageously doing exactly what God has planned.

Moms & Teen Girls Can Study Together!

Moms and teen girls can study and memorize God's Word together! Both *10 Scriptures to Know by Heart* workbooks have the same ten Bible verses but with tailor made and age relevant devotions and activities to speak to the individual heart.

Additional Books by JJ Gutierrez

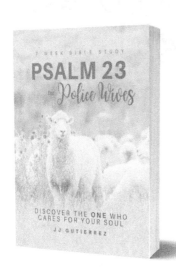

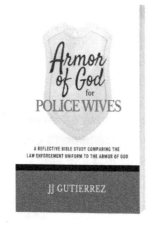

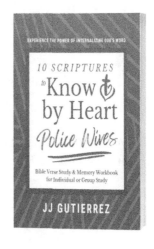

"Your Word is a lamp to my feet and a light to my path."

Psalm 119:105

For more information please connect at:

www.jjgutierrezauthor.com
www.instagram.com/jjgutierrezauthor
hello@jjgutierrezauthor.com

If you enjoyed this book, please consider leaving a review on Amazon. Reviews make a big difference in helping to get this book out to more women just like you!

Made in the USA
Las Vegas, NV
16 November 2024

11944811R00079